Cats

THEMES IN ART

Cats

JOHN NASH

SCALA BOOKS

Text © John Nash 1992
© Scala Publications Ltd and Réunion des
Musées Nationaux 1992

First published 1992
by Scala Publications Limited
3 Greek Street
London W1V 6NX

in association with
Réunion des Musées Nationaux
49 rue Etienne Marcel
Paris 75039

Distributed in the USA and Canada by
Rizzoli International Publications, Inc.
300 Park Avenue South
New York
NY 10010

ISBN 1 85759 009 0

Designed by Roger Davies
Edited by Paul Holberton
Produced by Scala Publications Ltd
Filmset by August Filmsetting, St Helens,
England
Printed and bound in Italy by Graphicom,
Vicenza

Photo credits: © ADAGP/SPADEM 1992
32, 34, 37; Bridgeman 7; G. Costa 14; ©
DACS 1992 34, 37; Giraudon 5, 28; Luciano
Pedicini 2; © RMN 17, 21, 22, 34, 37

**FRONTISPIECE   1 Medieval
artist**
*Mattathias beheading an
idolatrous Jew before a cat
idol*, **detail from the
Winchester Bible, folio 350v**
**Drawing on parchment
Winchester, Cathedral Library**

TITLE PAGE   Detail and whole of **8** Peter Paul
Rubens and Jan Brueghel the Elder,
The Fall of Man

THIS PAGE   **36** Franz Marc, *Three cats*

Contents

2　Pompeian artist
Tabby cat with a bird, 1st century A.D.
Mosaic, 51 × 51 cm
Naples, Museo Archeologico Nazionale
The cat is about to pull the partridge down from an upper shelf where it must have been placed on return from the market (it is still alive, with its legs tied). On the lower shelf sit two ducks, small fish strung together through their gills, oysters and sparrows, all alive and awaiting the cook's attention.

Egypt, Rome and the Bible

The cat, idolized in ancient Egypt, has been permitted only a minor role in European art. That is not to say cats do not appear in paintings. They certainly do, if not nearly so frequently as dogs. But between Egyptian statues of the cat-goddess Bastet and the twentieth century, cats have seldom been the sole or single subject of a painting. Instead they have played a supporting and often symbolic role, commenting in one way or another on the main scene.

The domestic cat is an immigrant to Europe, first crossing the Mediterranean in the company of traders and then gaining the outer reaches of the Roman Empire as a camp follower of the legions. It is already unmistakably at home in a Roman mosaic from the House of the Faun in Pompeii, now in the Museo Nazionale in Naples (**1**), showing a mackerel tabby holding a partridge under its paw. It is a cat that appears already to have established itself in what has remained its domain: the kitchen. For this cat has not caught its prey for itself: the fowl's legs are tied.

This design was sufficiently popular to have survived in more than one version, and may be derived from a Greek prototype. Technically it is a skilful achievement and calls to mind Pliny's report of the second-century B.C. mosaicist, Sosus of Pergamum, who was the first to lay an illusionistic floor in a dining room. On it were represented, as if dropped from the table, chicken and fish bones, the claws of shellfish, half-eaten fruit, nutshells and pips. The form became popular and was associated with the work of an ancient Greek painter, Piraikos, who painted similar scraps as still lifes and became known as a ropographer, or painter of trifles. As he also painted subjects considered sordid, this quickly became rhyparographer, painter of indecencies. The Romans admired such works and the tabby with the fowl is only one of many similar motifs repeatedly used in decorative mosaics.

Then, for almost a millennium and a half, the cat leaves few traces in the arts of Western Europe. As a small intruder into the kitchens and cloisters of the monasteries of early Christendom, the cat was associated with the idolatry of ancient Egypt. There, the fertility goddess Bastet had been represented as a cat or a cat-headed woman holding a sistrum, a percussion instrument. The Greek historian Plutarch explained that the roundness of the sistrum represented the moon while its sides symbolized the horns of Hathor, a goddess represented as a cow. It has been suggested that the image of Bastet with her sistrum lies behind the English nursery rhyme:

> Hey diddle diddle, the cat and the fiddle,
> The cow jumped over the moon.

A cat playing a fiddle on the lower margin of a medieval manuscript (British Library, MS Harl. 6563, f.40) is among the earliest Western paintings of cats.

Medieval Christian awareness of the idolatrous character of Egyptian sculptures of cats is more directly reflected in the twelfth-century Winchester Bible. The frontispiece to the apocryphal Book of Maccabees shows Mattathias beheading an infidel as he worships at the shrine of a cat-headed idol (**2**). This was at the time when the Cathars (adherents of the heretical Christian sect of the Languedoc who styled themselves from the Greek *katharos* meaning "pure") were said to be so-called because they worshipped the devil in the form of a cat.

3 Medieval artist
'Mousers' or *cats*, from a bestiary of *c*1250
Illumination on parchment, MS Bodley 764, folio 51
Oxford, Bodleian Library
The text reads: "She is called MOUSER
because she is fatal to mice. The vulgar call her
CATUS because she catches things[acaptura]
while others say that it is because she lies in
wait [captat], i.e. because she 'watches'. So
acutely does she glare that her eye penetrates
the shades of darkness with a gleam of light.
Hence from the Greek catus, i.e. 'acute'."

Twelfth-century writers of bestiaries (the
natural histories of the time), working in the
libraries of monasteries, had little to say about
the cat. Their authorities on natural history,
Aristotle and Pliny, had almost nothing to tell
them. Aristotle briefly described the mating
behavior of cats and added that the female cat
is particularly lecherous and weedles the male
on to sexual commerce and catawauls during
the operation.

The function of the bestiary was not so
much the accumulation of information on
animal behavior but its theological interpretation. On the dog, the bestiarist had much to
report. Much could be learned from its habits.
For example, priests are like watchdogs. They
drive away the trespassing devil when he
threatens to steal God's treasures, that is,
human souls. Again, a dog can cure a wound
by licking it, and in the same way a priest will
cleanse the wounded soul of a sinner by the
penance imposed at confession. The penance
will serve as a good licking. But on the cat, the
bestiarist had almost nothing to say. The cat
catches mice, lies in wait, has luminous eyes
and, most significantly, is called "she" (**3**). It is,
most probably, this female character, posses-
sed by all cats whatever their actual sex, that
made them such equivocal companions in the
monastery and indeed elsewhere. The bestiarist makes no mention of the cat's less desir-
able attributes. He had no need: the
identification of the cat as female made it
unnecessary to do so. The weaknesses of
woman were fully documented in the third
chapter of the Book of Genesis.

This is what makes the appearance of a cat
harnessed to draw an ape in the margin
(where the most abandoned of images might
flourish) of Psalm 80 in a psalter of about 1300
in Jesus College, Oxford (**4**), so significant.
Cats appear rarely even among the grotesques in the margins of medieval manuscript

illuminations. Dogs are six times as plentiful, and hares occur half as many times again as dogs. But the creature most likely to be discovered in the foliage proliferating in the margins of a psalter or book of hours is the ape. Apes are six times as common as dogs, four times as frequent as hares. These apes were in the margins because they had no place within the sacred text and the images it embraced. Apes were literally obscene. They aped humanity in particular and all goodness in general. Apes (for which the Latin was *simia*) offered "similitudes" that were seductive in their false equivalences. Apes were of the devil's party, if not images of the devil himself. The devil himself aped God. For the ape to have harnessed the cat demonstrates his hold over her. It recalls the ancient fable in which the ape used the cat's paw to pull chestnuts from the fire.

Otherwise, on her rare appearances in the margins of medieval manuscripts, the cat, as might have been expected from the bestiarist's account, is most often seen with a mouse in her jaws. Cats were intruders into human society. They could not be owned. They entered the house by stealth, like mice, and were suffered because they kept the insufferable mice in check.

4   Medieval artist
Harnessed cat pulling a monkey, from a psalter of *c*1300
Illumination on parchment, MS Jesus College D40, folio 110
Oxford, Bodleian Library
Here the cat appears in the margin of a psalter (at Psalm 80) just as it was deemed to inhabit the margins of human society, and to belong to the lower world of foolery and the flesh.

Domestication

Possibly the earliest moment in painting that the cat's place in the household is recognized is in the *Très Riches Heures* of Jean, duc de Berri, illuminated for him by the Limbourg brothers between 1413 and 1416. There, in the month of February (5) a hardly recognizable white cat curls by the fire.

This scene is remarkable in several respects. The representations in the *Très Riches Heures* of the months of the year are themselves novel. In earlier books of hours, each month had been represented by a single human figure engaged in the appropriate activity of the month. But in their book of hours for the duc de Berri, instead of a single figure engaged in a representative labor, the Limbourg brothers provided a landscape replete with the activities of each month, reflecting the social conditions not simply of their time, but of their patron.

The duc de Berri was, in his day, one of the richest men in the world. He owned ten castles. From March to December, the Limbourg brothers set the labors—and recreations—of the month within the domain of one of the duc's châteaux. For January and February they adopted a different approach. January, for which traditionally the two-faced Roman god Januarius (or Janus) was shown feasting and facing past and future at the turning of the year, revealed Jean, duc de Berri himself feasting luxuriously within one of his châteaux, his hounds around him and lap dogs even on the table. February was the polar opposite of this festive scene. The traditional image for February had been a peasant, bootless, warming himself by his fire. The Limbourgs show not simply that but the sheep huddling in their stalls, beehives shrouded in snow, a peasant woman muffled in a cloak, blowing on her frozen fingers, a peasant urging on an ass laden with sticks for fuel, magpies searching for food, and a glimpse of another entire village suffering from cold beyond the hill. This is the world of the peasant in winter. And in the bottom left-hand corner, which for another two-and-a-half centuries would remain a favored place for Northern painters to insert the key motif in their pictures, is the original image of the peasant warming himself. Not one peasant but three sit before the fire, their sole, small luxury (the duc's fire, indicated in January, is immense and he protects himself from its heat by a great circular wicker screen). The better to appreciate the meager warmth, the peasants, male and female, hoist their skirts, comically exposing their genitals. And here the cat finds a place among the peasants, akin to their low estate.

The cat will stay by the fire—that is her elected place—but, about a century later, she appears to have advanced socially. In an early sixteenth-century book of hours, now in the Pierpont Morgan Library, New York, much has changed. The man warming himself at the fire in January has the bulk of a successful merchant and wears a fur-lined coat as he sits before an enormous blaze in a room luxurious with wainscot and shuttered windows. A second room, the kitchen, with a second blazing fire can be seen through the open door. It is a scene with many telling details. A small bird is in a cage hanging against the chimneybreast, a metal chandelier hangs from the rafters and a woman, the housewife, is bringing a roast leg of lamb to the table. A large jug, probably of ale, can be glimpsed at the merchant's right hand. And on his left, not lurking beneath a cupboard or under a chair but accepted, sitting boldly upright and also basking before the fire, is a handsome cat.

5 The Limbourg brothers
The month of February, from the *Très Riches Heures* of Jean, duc de Berri, 1413–16
Illumination on parchment, 29 × 26 cm
Chantilly, Musée Condé

By contrast to January, where the duc is shown with his dogs before an enormous fire, in this image representing February the peasants are shown warming themselves before a small fire with their ignoble cat.

Detail of 5

Eve and the cat

The early image of bourgeois luxury in the Pierpont Morgan manuscript bears no apparent moral significance, unlike an otherwise comparable interior with a cat painted at much the same time by Hieronymus Bosch (6). There can be no doubt about the implication of this scene. It is inscribed *Superbia* (Pride) and the scene is only a detail in a larger painting, the *Table of the Seven Deadly Sins*. On this large rectangular panel, displayed horizontally like a table, is inscribed a great circle containing two smaller concentric circles. The two inner circles resemble an eye. In the pupil Christ the Man of Sorrows stands in a sarcophagus with the inscription: "Beware, beware, the Lord sees." The iris is a sheaf of golden rays extending to illuminate the worldly activities revealed in the outer circle. This is divided into seven compartments within each of which is shown one of the sins.

Bosch represents the sins as enacted by his contemporaries. Different classes and occupations have different temptations: *Gula* (Greed) is the sin of the poor; *Luxuria* (Lust) of the nobility; *Invidia* (Envy) is the sin of the merchant; *Ira* (Anger) that of drunken boers. Pride is exemplified by the burgher's wife adorning herself. She is not even aware of being tempted into vanity by the devil who holds up the glass for her. Beyond, in the kitchen by the blazing fire, another figure, too, looks into a mirror. Between them Bosch has placed a cat. In his didactic poem *The Ship of Fools* (1497), Sebastian Brandt likened the adulterous wife to a cat. Just as the cat was never content with a single mouse, so the woman would never be satisfied by a single adultery. The cat is "she", the figure of woman and necessarily kin with the first of women, Eve, as the scholars in the monasteries well knew. It is close by Eve that

Hieronymus Bosch again includes a cat in the left wing of his *Garden of Earthly Delights* triptych (7). The scene Bosch depicts appears to be based on Genesis 2,22, and shows God, having created Eve from Adam's rib, introducing her to Adam. It is before the serpent has tempted Eve to tempt Adam, to cause the Fall of Man and the sin that dominates the central panel of the triptych, but already the cat is strolling away with a mouse in her jaws.

A cat was placed at the feet of Eve by Albrecht Dürer in his engraved *Fall of Man* of 1504. Erwin Panofsky explained its presence by associating it with the elk, ox and rabbit also included. Each creature, he said, represented one of the four humors or temperaments that made up a man. The elk denoted melancholic gloom, the ox phlegmatic sluggishness, the rabbit sanguine sensuality and the cat choleric cruelty. Man before his Fall had been an immortal, balanced compound of all four humors. With the first sin he fell into mortality and, henceforth, no man was perfectly tempered but each was dominated, like all mortal flesh, by one or other humor. This explanation has been generally accepted, though Dürer's animals do not match in any instance the quartet that more usually represented the humors: the pig for melancholy, the lamb for phlegm, the ape for sanguineness

6   Hieronymus Bosch
Pride, **detail of the** *Table of the Seven Deadly Sins*, **1490**
Oil on panel, 120 × 150 cm (whole)
Madrid, Prado
In this detail the late medieval association of the cat with vanity, sensuality and sex is clear: the cat is present as the sinful associate of that most intrinsically sinful of God's creatures, woman.

superbia

7   Hieronymus Bosch
Adam and Eve in the Garden of Eden,
from the *Garden of Earthly Delights*
triptych, after 1500
Oil on panel, 220 × 97 cm
Madrid, Prado

Bosch, it is said, saw evil everywhere,
and so even in the Garden of Eden
placed a cat in the process of hunting
and killing. More plausibly the cat
catching the mouse is there as a
symbol, as a kind of premonition of
the catching of Adam by Eve when
she offers him an apple. Its presence
suggests that their innocence cannot
last.

Detail of 7

and the lion for choler. A lion would not have been out of place in the Garden of Eden, and, indeed, appears there in later representations such as one by Jan Brueghel the Elder and Peter Paul Rubens (**8**). But it is a cat that Brueghel, like Dürer, like Bosch and like Cornelis Cornelisz van Haarlem (**9**), places close by Eve.

Brueghel's cat rubs against Eve's legs—or, rather: *one* of the cats there rubs against Eve, for its mate watches beadily from a nearby tree. The moment represented is, of course, that instant when Adam succumbs to Eve's temptation and so, through woman's cunning, discovers not only sexual knowledge but death. In his version of this awful moment, Cornelis van Haarlem places a cat not rubbing against Eve but behind her and in the embrace of a monkey. Again the ape uses the cat's paw to rake the chestnuts from the fire. Ape and cat are similitudes of the serpent and of Eve who is here the cat's paw to catch Adam.

The cat as Eve finds an echo in Edward Topsell's *Historie of Foure-footed Beasts* of 1607, where he records that cats and serpents love one another. He relates that monks in a certain monastery fell sick because they used to play with the abbey-cat who also played with a serpent which "had emptied some of her poyson vppon the cat which brought the same to the Monkes, and they by stroking and handeling the cat, were infected therewith."

A quite different aspect of the cat's association with Eve survives in the folklore of the cat's love of woolen yarn (reflected not only in Lewis Carroll's *Through the Looking Glass* but in countless *New Yorker* cartoons). After the Expulsion from Paradise, while Adam delved, Eve, of course, span. Spinning became the occupation of the chaste spinster and virtuous wife. A cat playing with a spindle, the essential attribute of the spinster, sometimes

8   Peter Paul Rubens and Jan Brueghel the Elder
The Fall of Man, 1615
Oil on panel 74 × 114 cm
The Hague, Mauritshuis

Among the colorful parade of animals in the Garden of Eden, including a lion, one cat appears in close association with Eve, already her pet. But another cat, probably her mate, waits some distance away beside a tree, not nearly so tame. Undoubtedly an element of menace hung about this creature, more famous for hunting than for her sociability.

18

appears in the margins of twelfth-century manuscripts. Again, a woman chasing a cat with her distaff also appears as a marginal figure.

Cats show a particular affinity with spinning and weaving. A cat playing with a ball of wool has crept, most unusually, into the foreground of Pintoricchio's fresco of *Scenes from the Odyssey*, now in the National Gallery, London (**10**). The cat sits at the base of Penelope's loom and may, for once, indicate Penelope's virtue. Again, a cat accompanying a woman spinning is unique among the works produced by Raphael and his workshop. The occasion was a light-hearted decoration in the loggietta frescoed for cardinal Bibbiena in the Vatican, the first of a number of loggie in the Vatican decorated by Raphael with grotesques.

Another Italian cat associated with weaving also appears in a fresco decoration. This is the curious series, now in the National Gallery, London (**11**), that Domenichino painted in the Aldobrandini Villa Belvedere at Frascati in about 1605, to mimic tapestries. The tapestry of *Apollo slaying the Cyclops* is represented as having its bottom right edge turned up to expose the wall and floor against which it hangs. There, beside a life-sized chained dwarf and among debris that includes apples and a plate with chicken bones, sits a cat with a bird in its mouth. Like Raphael's loggietta, this facetious contrast between the images within the tapestry which are the traditional subjects of high art and the marginal low subjects of dwarf, cat and detritus, is a learned joke. It was probably intended to recall the rhyparography of Piraikos and the illusionistic mosaics of Sosus of Pergamum, in the manner of the Roman mosaic cat and fowl. A seventeenth-century Spanish painting that not only associates a cat with weaving and tapestry but, like the Domenichino, makes the contrast

9   Cornelis Cornelisz van Haarlem
The Fall of Man, 1592
Oil on canvas 273 × 220 cm
Amsterdam, Rijksmuseum

In the embrace of a monkey, the cat is presented as a devilish figure, intimating that evil is being committed. The association of cat and ape goes back to the early Middle Ages (see 4), and recalls the fable in which the ape used the paw of the cat to pull a chestnut from the fire.

10   Pintoricchio
Scenes from the Odyssey, 1509
Fresco transferred to canvas, 126 × 152 cm
London, National Gallery

Penelope was a heroine of unassailable virtue.
She waited faithfully twenty years for her
husband's return, and deceived the suitors who
would take his place by telling them she would
re-marry only when she had finished weaving a
winding-sheet for her father-in-law, which,
however, she unpicked again at night. So for
once the cat appears here beside her without
any evil suggestion.

11   Domenichino
Apollo slaying the Cyclops, c1617
Fresco transferred to canvas, 361.3 × 190.4 cm
London, National Gallery

Probably Domenichino has deliberately
revived the classical tradition of
"rhyparography" or "indecency painting," by
providing a glimpse of low life behind his
mythological curtain. This cat, then, is a
Renaissance copycat of ancient Greek and
Roman subjects such as the mosaic tabby from
Pompeii (2).

between the universally significant histories of high art and the universality of the daily round is Velázquez's painting of the story of Arachne, now known as *Las Hilanderas* or *The weavers*, in the Prado. However, this association with the chaste occupations of spinning and weaving does not appear to have redeemed the cat sufficiently to make her acceptable in images of the new Eve, sent to overcome original sin, that is, the Virgin Mary; the cat does not appear even in scenes of her early education in which the Virgin was often shown embroidering or making lace, and where the company of a cat might have been acceptable.

There is an Italian legend of *il gatto della Madonna*, the cat of the Madonna, who on the first Christmas Day produced a litter in the stable as the Virgin bore the Christ Child and who in consequence was marked with a cross on her back. But this does not appear in the works of any outstanding painter. Leonardo da Vinci did make a number of drawings of a Holy Family in which the Christ Child hugs a cat, but he never made the painting.

In his *Annunciation* (**12**), Lorenzo Lotto, often a painter of eccentric images, shows a cat startled by the appearance of the angel Gabriel. This has been explained as the devil fleeing from the imminent incarnation, but also as an image of Mary's fertility. Neither interpretation is convincing. It is more probable that the cat, creature of the old Eve, is dismissed as Mary accepts her role as the new Eve.

In an *Annunciation* in the National Gallery of Art, Washington, Paolo Veronese includes a cat that is plainly unperturbed by the presence not only of the angel Gabriel but of God the Father supported and accompanied by ranks of angels. Even the dove-like form of the Holy Spirit does not distract this cat from the saucer of milk over which she crouches.

Almost a century later, Rembrandt placed a cat close to the Virgin Mary, in his *Holy Family with a curtain*, now in Kassel (**13**). This panel might show a contemporary family at home: only the father at work as a carpenter and the familiarity of pictorial tradition serve to identify the subject. The family is poor, the house without a separate hearth, and beside the small fire, burning not in a grate or hearth but directly on the floor, a cat crouches in its typical, familiar way. Is this an example of Rembrandt's often remarked indifference to pictorial traditions? Possibly it is. But in an etching he made showing a similar interior in which the Virgin and Child are also accompanied by a cat, Rembrandt certainly followed Italian Catholic pictorial imagery. Beneath the Virgin's foot writhes a serpent, an established image identifying the Virgin as the new Eve crushing the serpent under her foot. So is the cat, here, redeemed by its association with the new Eve or is it a reminiscence of the old Eve? The cat may also have a deeper significance: she is staring at a small earthenware porringer with a spoon in it placed on the floor beside the fire. The Virgin is weaning the Christ Child. Weaning is another consequence of Christ's incarnation. Will the cat, lover of cream and most carnal of creatures, share the remains of that milky meal?

12 Lorenzo Lotto
The Annunciation, c1527
Oil on panel, 166 × 114 cm
Recanati, Pinacoteca Comunale
The Venetian painter Lorenzo Lotto was fond both of pseudo-hieroglyphic symbols and of touches of realism. This cat is both a realistic touch and a meaningful symbol—a wonderful example of the literal way in which Lotto imagined spiritual happenings. Undoubtably, if the Virgin had had a cat, the cat would have been frightened by the angel Gabriel.

23

13 Rembrandt van Rijn
The Holy Family, 1646

Oil on panel, 46.5 × 68.8 cm
Kassel, Gemäldegalerie

To a greater degree than any painter before
him, Rembrandt depicted religious subjects
afresh, as if they were happening in his own
place and time. That does not mean that he
divested the elements in his pictures of their
traditional associations, and the cat which here
shares the life of this simple peasant family
may well hint at the role of the Virgin as the
new Eve.

Detail of 13

The cat in Venice

Feasts provided the few New Testament subjects in which cats were acceptable, and even there, sixteenth-century Italian painters seldom chose to include them. Two who did, Paolo Veronese and his contemporary Tintoretto, were both Venetian, which is not surprising, for Venice is a city of cats.

Veronese painted a number of feasts in which he set cats. In his grand painting, now in the Louvre, of the *Feast at Cana*, the occasion of Christ's first miracle when he turned water into wine, a cat clings to a wine-cooler in the right foreground. This vast work was appropriately commissioned to decorate the refectory of San Giorgio Maggiore in Venice. Veronese received many such commissions. The *Last Supper* was a favorite subject for such situations, but Veronese appears to have found the *Feast at Cana* more congenial.

In 1573, Veronese was summoned before the tribunal of the Inquisition to explain the inclusion of unsuitable elements in a painting of the *Feast in the house of Simon* intended for the refectory of Santi Giovanni e Paolo in Venice. The charge was serious: if established it would have amounted to blasphemy. Veronese replied: "We painters take the same license as the poets and jesters take." The outcome was that "the above named Paolo would be obliged to improve and change his painting within a period of three months from the day of this admonition" at his own expense or be liable to the penalties imposed by the holy tribunal. The painting, in the Accademia, Venice, is still known as *Christ in the house of Levi* and though no penitent harlot washes Christ's feet, a cat, similitude of a sinful woman, crouches there in her stead.

In the painting of the same subject in the Brera, Milan (**14**), Veronese does represent the anointing of Christ's feet by a penitent Magdalene, and places the action at the extreme left of his horizontally extended canvas. In the center of the canvas, between the two tables given to the feast, and in the foreground he shows two hounds setting about a cat. Again, this cat may represent the fallen woman, the two hounds the disciples who had condemned her actions.

Tintoretto painted numerous versions of the *Last Supper* and of the preceding *Christ washing the disciples' feet*, and in several he placed a cat lurking about the table. In *Christ washing the disciples' feet* in the National Gallery, London, the poor cat placed prominently on the perspective pattern of the tiled floor leading to the fire has been reduced by time and restoration to little more than a suggestive silhouette. But in the *Last Supper* in San Giorgio Maggiore in Venice (**15**), one of the finest cats in painting is placed strikingly in the foreground. This great painting is an astonishing invention. It is all pictorial pyrotechnics and spiritual vision. The lamp suspended from the ceiling is supplemented by the light emitted by the eleven small halos of the disciples and all these sources are subordinate to the blinding glory emanating from the head of Christ. Following the Gospel according to St Luke, Christ stands to offer the disciples the bread that is his body while on the wrong side of the long trestle table sits Judas. He is isolated on the side of the carnal, the mortal, the side of the servants, the food and, in the foreground, directly below Christ but inevitably indifferent to his momentous action, the cat, engrossed in the contents of a wicker basket from which a servant extracts provisions.

14   Paolo Veronese
Christ in the house of Simon, c1570
Oil on canvas, 275 × 710 cm
Milan, Brera

The cat being attacked by two dogs may have been placed so prominently in the foreground to reflect the situation of the sinner attacked by the disciples when she annoints Christ's feet at this banquet, two days before the Crucifixion.

15   Jacopo Tintoretto
The Last Supper, 1592–94
Oil on canvas, 365 × 568 cm
Venice, San Giorgio Maggiore

The cat appears once more as the denizen of
the kitchen, among the servants who prepare
the meal and bring on its courses. The cat
seems to have decided to look into the basket
after the serving-girl has pulled from it a bowl
of sweatmeats she offers to another servant.
She may not have long to find out what is in it,
because a dog, who by contrast has been
among the diners at the table, has caught sight
of her. Whether or not this has any symbolic
significance, the cat and dog have the pictorial
role, like the gestures of the figures, of leading
the eye from point to point round the painting,
and then back to its center, Christ.

Overleaf: detail of 15

The cat in the Low Countries

The contrast between the spiritual and the carnal seen in the *Last Supper* in San Giorgio Maggiore recurs in the paintings of two of Tintoretto's Flemish contemporaries. In the Netherlands, Pieter Aertsen and Joachim Bueckelaer painted a number of kitchen interiors in the background of which a small scene from Christ's ministry was set. A favorite choice was Christ in the house of Martha and Mary (Luke, 10, 38–42), when Christ rebuked Martha for being "cumbered with much serving," unlike her sister who sat to listen to his spiritual teaching. The relation between foreground kitchen and background gave visual representation to the contrast of physical and spiritual that was Christ's teaching.

Cats might well have been expected to insinuate themselves into such kitchens. On the contrary, they are remarkable by their absence. But a fine cat does appear in a similar scene by an eclectic Dutch painter of the following generation, Joachim Wtewael. Wtewael painted many bizarre, Mannerist versions of mythological subjects but his *Kitchen scene* of 1605, in Berlin, is an earthy continuation of the traditional Netherlandish treatment.

In the tradition of kitchen paintings, the flesh of the animal carcases was identified with sexual carnality. Wtewael makes the equation clear, not only in the gesture of the fair kitchen maid spitting the plucked chickens but also by the heated behavior of the couple by the fire. But beside the couple a child pauses from cleaning out a copper pot to watch a dog and a cat as they crouch with their eyes fixed on a dead fish on the floor between them. Wtewael's contemporary Karel van Mander identified the dog as the good teacher who

watches over the human spirit. The cat, by contrast, must, once again, represent the sins of the flesh.

Kitchen or market still lifes, large canvases filled with a display of uncooked carcases and vegetables, were painted throughout the seventeenth century. These canvases were seldom restricted to the market produce; there was usually a living presence. If a cook was not included, there would be a dog or a cat (or both). One of the most extravagantly outrageous versions of such a kitchen piece is a large canvas by Paul de Vos in the Prado (**16**). A careless pantry boy has left open a window, and no fewer than five cats are hurling themselves and tumbling through, fighting as they spill over the shelf among the vegetables, plucked fowl and canes loaded with small garden birds.

This was the tradition that Chardin revived in his grand painting *The ray* (**17**). It was one of a number of canvases that the young painter exhibited in 1728, on 3 June, the Feast of Corpus Christi, at the Place Dauphine where a number of members of the Académie Royale would see them. He was immediately invited to offer himself for membership of the Académie and on 25 September was accepted without demur. *The ray* is one of Chardin's largest and boldest canvases, painted in a distinctively Netherlandish manner. The color is subdued, dominated by the almost monochrome umbers of the rear stone wall. The low tones of the jug and pans on the right are hardly distinguished one from another, yet the objects have individual solidarity and volume and clearly are set apart in space. It is a *tour de force* of painterly skills. The ray, hung in the center, and the fish and oysters on the shelf below have tempted the cat. It balances

16 Paul de Vos
Cat fight in the kitchen, 17th century
Oil on canvas, 116 × 172 cm
Madrid, Prado

In this study the leaping, scrabbling cats have taken over the kitchen, in the absence of the cook. Although these kitchen scenes began as moralizations on a theme from the Bible, increasingly they became exercises in the painterly skill of still life. The cat, who typically haunts the larder, becomes a part of the still life and occasionally, as here, becomes its main focus.

Detail of 16

17   Jean-Baptiste-Siméon Chardin
The ray, 1728
Oil on canvas, 114.5 × 146 cm
Paris, Louvre

This 18th-century French still life belongs in
the tradition of the 17th-century Dutch kitchen
piece, of which the cat was an element. It is
suggested that the cat has been alarmed by the
apparent menace of the illusion of a face in the
belly of the ray, but it is more likely to have
been surprised, alarmed and thwarted by a
returning servant.

Detail of 17

precariously upon the open oysters, its back arched, its eyes fixed in a downward stare.

The medieval bestiarist had identified only two attributes of the cat: she caught mice and had acute vision. Edward Topsell, in 1607, noted that "her eies glister above measure especialy when a man commeth to see a cat on a sudden, and in the night, they can hardly be endured, for their flaming aspect ... they cast forth beames in the shaddow and darkenes" and so can see perfectly at night to kill rats and mice. Thus the cat was the appropriate creature to exemplify the sense of sight. In prints showing the five senses, each sense was personified as a woman holding an appropriate object or attribute and accompanied by a creature noted for possessing that sense. Sight always holds a mirror as her attribute and, in earlier allegorical treatments, her animal was usually an eagle, the only creature with eyes strong enough to stare into the sun. But an eagle would have been incongruous within the domestic settings of Dutch imagery of the seventeenth century and the cat was preferred.

This is not to claim that the cat in Dutch painting is symbolic. In the new realistic style of the seventeenth-century Netherlands an image of a woman holding a mirror and accompanied by a cat *recalls*, rather than *is*, a personification of sight. In the same spirit, it may also recall an image of vanity, pride or even Venus at her toilet. And if these associations come to mind, then reminiscences of the cat's other notorious propensities may follow. As Aristotle had noted, the she-cat had an insatiable lust, and the recollection of this might, in its turn, call to mind the simile, made by Sebastian Brandt in his *Ship of Fools*, of the cat and the adulterous wife.

But in all the vast quantity of scenes of contemporary life, of merry companies, outdoor parties, kermesses, fairs, inns, and the variety of domestic interiors, peasant and burgher, that were painted in seventeenth-century Holland, dogs are everywhere but there are remarkably few cats. This cannot be because cats were scarce. It must be that cats were still not regarded as part of the family. They were tolerated in the kitchen and beneath the table but they were still regarded as creatures of carnal sin.

Jan Molenaer, for example, has painted an allegorical portrait in which a young couple standing together on the right are faced by what seems to be a range of choices between virtue and vice (**18**). A young man in the center of the scene pours from one jug into another in an action symbolic of temperance while to the left another young man stares into a beer tankard with the equally stereotyped gesture of the drunkard. Meanwhile, in the foreground, a dog beside the couple looks askance at a monkey cuddling a cat or kitten. Here again is that traditional association of cat and ape not flattering to either. God's ape, the devil, had used Eve as his cat's paw to tempt man into sin. Furthermore, this ape is chained to a heavy block of timber, an established image of man enchained to his senses. There can be little doubt that as the two men symbolize temperance and indulgence, so the dog represents virtue while ape and cat denote vice.

Dutch painters so rarely set a cat in a scene

18   Jan Molenaer
Allegorical portrait of a family on a terrace, 1633
Oil on canvas, 99.1 × 140.9 cm
Richmond (VA), Museum of Art
By their actions, echoing the attributes of medieval tradition, the various figures are shown as virtuous or vicious. The cat continues in her role as a creature of sensuality, and is once more associated with her old evil and wily companion, the ape.

that its presence is suspicious. In a painting in the National Gallery, London, known as the *Idle servant* (**19**), Nicolaes Maes places his sleeping servant among unwashed dishes while behind her a cat makes off with a plucked fowl. The imagery seems calculated to recall the Dutch proverb: a kitchen maid must keep one eye on the pan and the other on the cat.

Again, a popular subject among Dutch painters was the doctor's visit. The patient was almost always a young woman, her trouble love's sickness: she was pregnant. In such a scene a dog was usually included, so when in his version, now in the Rijksmuseum, Samuel Hoogstraten includes a cat instead, the viewer is provoked to wonder why. Is this pregnancy the consequence of adultery?

Only in Jan Steen's paintings do cats lurk inconspicuously as is their habit in reality. In his work, the cat's presence seems often to add nothing to the significance of the scene. She may sit beneath a table behind a man offering a woman oysters (National Gallery, London) or under the table at which the peasant in Aesop's fable terrifies his guest the satyr because he can both warm his hands and cool his soup by blowing on them (Bredius Museum, The Hague). In inns, cottages, and burgher homes, Steen seems to include cats because he likes them.

Nevertheless, in some paintings Steen, too, gives the cat a specific and significant role. In the large painting in the Mauritshuis, sometimes known as the *Inn of the World*, a child tries to teach a kitten to dance on its hind legs: an example of a vain and therefore foolish attempt to educate the ineducable (as Aristotle observed, the cat's small face betrays a small mind). In *The effects of intemperance* in the National Gallery, London, children encourage a cat to gorge itself on pie. The significance of the "family of cats," in Steen's

Detail of 19

19   Nicholas Maes
The idle servant, 1655
Oil on panel, 70 × 53.3 cm
London, National Gallery
This painting is a depiction not simply of idleness but of sensuality; it is related to other Dutch kitchen scenes where the pile of heaped food is a symbol of vanity and distraction from God. At the same time it illustrates the real consequences of a lack of vigilance—the cat gets up to mischief.

Detail of 20

20 Jan Steen
"The family of cats", 1670s
Oil on canvas, 150 × 148 cm
Budapest, Szépmüvészeti Muzeum
The adult cat is being shown a litter of kittens
in a basket by two young women, who are
accompanied by two young men, one of them
bending over the basket and playing a flute.
The people are evidently teasing the cat, which
is distinctly angry. Its movement as it wriggles
in the girl's grasp is convincingly painted,
although its expression is exaggerated and
anthropomorphic. This "low-life" scene is
probably a moralizing picture representing
base instincts, human and animal.

painting in Budapest (**20**), now often given
that title, is far from clear. The painting is large
and ambitious, of the type known as a Merry
Company. It has been suggested that the
pleasures of the five senses are symbolized
here, and that the stroking of the cats represents touch. That many of the details in the
painting are symbolic cannot be doubted. The
activity is set between the wine barrel in the
foreground and the glass raised by the bag-
pipe player in the rear, and once again appears
to represent the effects of intemperance. The
skull on a shelf above the bagpipes is a
memento mori. The captive owl on the extreme
left signifies stupidity: though able to see at
night the owl is blind in the day. Cats, too, can
see in the dark. Here is not a single cat, however, but a litter of five kittens in a basket and
an adult cat struggling to escape from a young
woman's arms and join them. What does it
want to do to the kittens? Edward Topsell in
1607 had written that the male cat is "most
libidinous, and therefore seeing the female
will never more engender with him, during
the time hir young ones suck, hee killeth and
eateth them if he meet with them (to prouoke
the female to copulation with him againe, for
when she is depriued of her young she seeketh
out the male of her own accord)."

39

21   The Le Nain brothers
A peasant family, c1640/45
Oil on canvas, 113 × 159 cm
Paris, Louvre

The peasant subjects for which the Le Nain
brothers were famous differ from those by
contemporaries such as Adriaen Brouwer, the
Ostade brothers, or David Teniers by their
calm, stolid dignity. Their peasants are shown
in none of the usual antics in which these more
satirizing painters painted them. So, too, the
cats they place beside their peasants in many of
their paintings are quiet, companionable beasts,
depicted with affection.

Detail of 21

The cat as friend

There is one pictorial environment in the first half of the seventeenth century where a cat appears to have been welcome for its own sake. This is not in the Netherlands but in Paris, in the paintings of the Le Nain brothers. The work of the Le Nain brothers is unusual in several ways. There is, initially, the curious matter of their being three brothers from a village, Laon, in Picardy, who turned not north but to Paris, arriving to set up as painters around 1629. Then there is the lack of records about their careers and there is the uncertainty about which of them painted individual pieces. It is not known whether they specialized in separate genres or collaborated on individual works of whatever genre. Finally, the paintings of peasants and peasant life that came from their hands have a distinctive and enigmatic character.

While other contemporary painters of peasant life condescended to their subjects, the Le Nain did not. Nor do the Le Nain show their peasants engaged in typical activity such as brawling, drinking, or playing cards. Their paintings have the character of group portraits in which the peasants pose with a solemn dignity that matches contemporary group portraits of Amsterdam burghers.

And of the two dozen or so scenes of peasant life that may safely be attributed to the Le Nain workshop, there is a cat in seven. No other painter for two hundred years treated a cat not only with the affection that this preference appears to display, but also with such dignity. For the Le Nain treated a cat as seriously as they treated a peasant woman. Nor did they restrict their celebrations of simple dignity to a small scale. Though many of these scenes are the expected "cabinet" size of a low-life subject, one painting in the Louvre (**21**) is over a meter and a half wide, which, while not heroic, is larger than virtually any canvas devoted to such a vulgar subject before Gustave Courbet painted his *Après diner à Ornans* that was so controversial in 1848.

In general, cats were acceptable in peasant scenes, inns and kitchens but in the seventeenth century still unsuitable for a bourgeois flower interior. However, they were seen as acceptable playthings for bourgeois children. Veronese even includes a child hugging a cat beneath a bench in a version of *The marriage at Cana* now in Dresden.

A more interesting early example of a child playing with a cat is in a large and elaborate group portrait painted by Otto van Veen, or Vaenius as he styled himself in the latinate mode of the day, a decade before he became the master of the young Peter Paul Rubens. Vaenius shows himself seated at his easel working on an allegory and surrounded by eighteen members of his family (**22**). Inscribed cartouches, left and right, testify to the importance the artist attached to this memorial of himself and his own. And in the foreground to the left is a white cat being affectionately stroked by a little girl, perhaps four years old. By coincidence, this was painted in 1584, not more than a half-dozen years after Michel Eyquem de Montaigne had written in his twelfth *essai*: "When I play with my cat, who knows whether she is not amusing herself with me more than I with her. We entertain each other with mutual monkeying: if I have my moment to play or not, she too has hers." Montaigne was, no doubt, a distinctive intellect, but his readiness not only to play with his cat but to confess to it and to recognize an equality between himself and the cat makes an

22   Vaenius (Otto van Veen)
The artist and his family, 1584
Oil on canvas, 165 × 250 cm
Paris, Louvre

This is a picture rare for its date in which the cat appears without moralizing overtones as a member of the family, as a family pet.
However, the cat is a pet for the children and not for the adults—there are records of adults playing with their cats, but it was regarded as a childish thing to do.

23   Judith Leyster
Two children with a cat and an eel (Allegory of Folly), 17th century
Oil on panel, 59.4 × 49 cm
London, National Gallery

The inane expressions of the children and the emphatic way they hold up the creatures they play with indicate that they represent examples of foolish, idle, and pointless behavior.

24 William Hogarth
The Graham children, 1742
Oil on canvas, 160.5 × 181 cm
London, National Gallery

It is likely that the cat is a portrait, too, like the children, but Hogarth has given it a dramatic and symbolic role that goes far beyond that of a friendly presence or a plaything. The cat's pursuit of the bird in the cage transforms the portrait from a static scene into a moment of turmoil, and at the same time recalls its old role as 'mouser' or predator in the Garden of Eden (8), harbinger of the end of these children's innocence.

Detail of 24

apt match to van Veen's inclusion of the family cat on equal terms with other members of his large family.

It was appropriate that children should play with cats, for childhood was the time for playing and cats were notoriously playful. This very playfulness could be dangerous. Edward Topsell remarked: "it is needelesse to spend any time about her loving nature to man, how she flattereth by rubbing her skinne against ones legges ... Therefore how she beggeth, playeth, leapeth ... riseth vp to strings held ouer her head ... is needlesse to standvpon; insomuch as Coelius was wont to say ... he was not ashamed to play and sport himselfe with his Cat, and verily it may well be called an idle mans pastime. As this beast has beene familiarly nourished of many, so have they payed deare for their loue, being requited with the losse of their health, and sometime of their life for their friendship." Because, Topsell informs his reader, "It is most certaine that the breath and sauour of cats consume the radicall humour and destroy the lungs, and therefore they which keepe their cats with them in their beds haue the aire corrupted and fall into feuer hectickes and consumptions." Playing, anyway, was not for adults but was to be left behind with childhood.

So when Judith Leyster paints a boy and smaller girl playing with a cat it is probable the image represents a foolish activity (23). The way the boy holds up an eel or slowworm while the girl looks knowingly at the viewer and holds up an admonitory finger suggests there is also a more precise symbolic significance but, so far, a convincing interpretation has not been proposed.

The splendid cat in Hogarth's portrait of the Graham children again has a role to play (24). The painting is an eccentric, ostentatious work: the figures are life-sized. It was commissioned by the children's father Daniel Graham,

25   Francisco Goya
Manuel Osorio Manrique de Zuñiga, c1786
Oil on canvas, 127 × 101.6 cm
New York, Metropolitan Museum of Art
The bird holds a card in its beak which gives it the resemblance of a fortune-teller's trained bird, but on the card there is no fortune given for the child, only a print of a bird and the artist's signature. The intent interest of the cats in the blithe and unaware bird does not, however, bode well, if they are to be read as an allegory of innocence and fate.

who was apothecary at the Chelsea Hospital, and it seems likely that Hogarth seized the opportunity (as he regularly did in his determination to establish a native school of English painting and himself at its head) to essay something rather grander that was really appropriate. Not only is this portrait rather larger than might have been expected, it is filled with symbolic details. On the clock to the left is the figure of Time indicating the brevity of childhood innocence and of life itself. The musical box, which is a serinette intended to teach caged birds to sing, is decorated with a relief of Orpheus charming the animals with his music. The bird being instructed is a goldfinch often painted in the hand of the Christ Child to represent man's immortal soul. And this is the object not only of the Graham son's attention but of the cat, which may be depicted from the family pet but is clearly intended by Hogarth to recall the imagery of man's fall and original sin.

In Spain, a little later, Goya included two cats in the portrait of an infant boy, Manuel Osorio Manrique de Zuñiga (25). Here, too, the cats have a most malign character as they crouch with their eyes fixed on the tethered but unconcerned magpie. In the second half of the eighteenth century, it became not only acceptable but even popular to have portraits of children holding a cat. In France, Perronneau's portrait of a girl with a kitten is not unique (26). Another similar piece is an oval painting by François Drouais (Paris, Musée Cognacq-Jay).

Thomas Gainsborough began a double portrait of his two daughters with a cat in the lap of one. He appears to have thought better of it and painted it out. He left the painting unfinished and, in time, the thin layer of paint he had wiped over the cat has become translucent and the cat is visible again. Later in his career, he painted a commissioned portrait of Miss Brummell, looking about seven years old, holding a kitten in her arms. This is now at Kenwood, and with it is a candle-light scene by Joseph Wright of Derby showing two girls dressing a kitten in doll's clothing that is totally in the tradition of seventeenth-century Dutch painting.

The new acceptability of a cat in the arms of a child recalls the observation of Christopher Smart: "My cat Joeffrey is an instrument for the children to learn benevolence on .... God be merciful to all dumb creatures in respect of pain."

26 Jean-Baptiste Perronneau
Girl with a kitten, 1745
Pastel on paper, 59 × 50 cm
London, National Gallery
Perhaps, once more, this kitten represents the old Eve long believed to be present in every woman, but there is an innocence here that presages our modern acceptance of the cat as a suitable companion for a child.

Lascivious cats

In France, in the eighteenth century, Chardin continued many of the traditions of seventeenth-century Dutch painting not only in still life but also in his scenes of daily life. *The laundresses*, in Stockholm, includes both a cat and a shabbily dressed boy blowing bubbles. This is appropriate enough in a wash house, but a boy blowing bubbles was also firmly established as an image of the brevity of all human life. Bubble-blowing not only represented a childish activity but also was a reminder of the necessity of putting such idleness behind one as the toiling washers had done. The cat, too, despite her famous cleanliness, was better known for her lust and her detestation of water and here may be seen as a contrast to the women engaged in their purifying activities.

Other French painters of the eighteenth century made the association unmistakable. In the previous century Dutch paintings of the morning toilet and other boudoir scenes had shown a lap dog as the familiar of the harlot. Eighteenth-century French erotica came to replace the dog with a cat, and the images leave little doubt of the sexual significance of the animal. François Boucher seldom painted cats, but on the half-dozen occasions that he did, several were in toilet scenes. In *La toilette*, in the Thyssen-Bornemisza collection (**27**), the significance of the position of the cat between the young woman's feet as she hoists up her skirts to adjust her garter is unmistakable. Boucher makes a similar association of cat and lap in another canvas in which a young man holds a rose under the nose of a cat seated in the lap of a sleeping peasant maid.

Lépicié's painting *The morning rising* (**28**) is directly derived from the Dutch tradition. The chamber pot, extinguished candle, shoes on the floor, even the broom (which was used by the harlot to sweep out the man once his resources were exhausted) and, above all, the woman's action of putting on her stocking, these are all taken directly from Dutch paintings of the morning toilet. The only innovations are the low-life poverty of the chamber and the cat to replace the dog.

In England, too, cats and prostitutes were synonymous by this time. In *The march to Finchley*, William Hogarth placed a row of cats along the gutter of a brothel from the windows of which the women hang out to attract the troops.

The cat in Nathaniel Hone's portrait of Kitty Fisher (National Portrait Gallery, London) is equally explicit. In the foreground, a black cat with white nose and paws hangs over the edge of a glass bowl fishing for goldfish. Kitty Fisher ignores this activity before her very nose. She artfully holds a tulle kerchief over her otherwise rather exposed bosom and looks the viewer straight in the eye. Kitty was a notoriously extravagant courtesan who once ate a twenty-pound note between two slices of bread. Her cat is a kindred spirit.

Again the kindred spirit of a prostitute is the cat in one of the most notorious paintings of the nineteenth century, Edouard Manet's *Olympia*. This was a modern version of Titian's famous *Venus of Urbino* in the Uffizi. Manet showed the Venus of modern Paris to be a shameless whore giving public audience while reclining naked on a throne-like divan. At her feet, where Titian had painted a spaniel, Manet placed a black cat. That Olympia is aware of the visitors to the annual Salon flocking to stare at her is confirmed by the cat

27 François Boucher
La toilette, 1730s
Oil on canvas, 52.5 × 66.5 cm
Lugano, Thyssen-Bornemisza Collection

In the seclusion of the boudoir, safe from
prying male eyes, this young woman raises her
skirts to adjust her garters, and there between
her exposed limbs nestles her pet cat. Popular
erotic prints of the period were less subtle.

28 Michel-Nicolas-Bernard Lépicié
The morning rising, 1773
Oil on canvas, 73.5 × 93 cm
Saint-Omer, Musée-Hôtel Sandelin

This is perhaps Lépicié's best-known painting, often called "Fanchon's rising" because it was believed to represent a Parisian street-singer who became proverbial and, later, the subject of a play. The play here is on the erotic symbols, among which the cat has a conspicuous role.

Detail of 28

which, like Chardin's cat caught with the ray, arches its back at the sight of intruders.

A cat first appeared in Manet's art in 1862, the year before he painted the *Olympia*, in a canvas that anticipates *Olympia* in other respects, too. This is a much smaller painting now in Yale (**29**), a little over half the width of the later picture, now known simply as *Young woman reclining in Spanish costume*. Though fully clothed, this young woman displays herself, or is displayed, erotically and, like *Olympia*, recalls an earlier painting of a nude. Her Spanish costume and her pose echo Goya's two paintings of a *maja*, clothed and nude: in effect, she combines them both, as the satin breeches are revealing in a way that contemporary women's costume was not. The reason for the cat on the floor beside the sofa is not immediately obvious—in this it is unlike the cat at Olympia's feet—and it could be a whimsical afterthought.

The subject of this portrait (for it has the character of a portrait) has not been identified. Because of the inscribed dedication to the photographer Nadar the painting has been said to represent his mistress. But it has also been claimed that the dedication was a later addition. This canvas is almost exactly the size of another canvas of the same year that depicts a woman reclining on a sofa, the portrait, now in Budapest, of Baudelaire's mistress, Jeanne Duval. Here there is no cat. Yet a connection is there. Baudelaire, like Manet, was fascinated by cats. He was delighted that Manet had put the black cat at the feet of *Olympia*. In *Les Fleurs du Mal* there are two poems called *Le chat*. One (LI) begins: "In my brain a beautiful cat strolls as if it were at home." Poem XXXIV tells his cat that when he strokes it he sees his mistress in his mind's eye. "Her look, like yours, fond beast, deep and cold, cuts and cleaves like a barb, and from head to foot, a subtle current, a perilous per-

fume, bathes her brown body." For Baudelaire, his mistress is a cat. If the Yale painting was painted as a pendant to this portrait of Jeanne Duval the inclusion of a cat would be most appropriate.

Manet added a cat but why did he add the orange, or rather two oranges? The woman's belly and thighs are subtly but unmistakably revealed by her clinging silky breeches: her small breasts are eclipsed by a black brassière. Perhaps this is because her breasts are more vividly represented on the floor. "*Elle a des oranges sur l'étagère*" ("she has oranges on her whatnot") was late nineteenth-century Parisian slang for "she has small breasts." The cat is playing with one and *chat* (cat) is a possible pun on *chatouiller* (to tickle): the words have a common origin (just as in Northern English dialect "the kittle kittles" means "the kitten tickles"). The question remains: if the dedication to Nadar was, indeed, added at a later date, who was tickling this *maja's* oranges in 1862?

Manet painted other cats. A black cat licks itself beneath the tail in the *Luncheon in the studio* of 1868 (Munich). A similarly occupied cat, conspicuously white, sits on the balcony in the view of Oloron Sainte-Marie now in the Bührle Collection. Manet sketched a portrait of Mme Manet in a pink peignoire with a black-and-white cat on her lap, now in the Tate Gallery, London.

In 1868, Manet drew a lithograph for a poster advertising a book on cats. The lithograph was a black-and-white drawing of a black and a white cat meeting on a Parisian rooftop. The book was *Les Chats, histoires, moeurs, anecdotes* by Champfleury. Illustrated with fifty-two designs taken from the works of such artists as "E. Delacroix, Brueghel, Violet-le-Duc, Ed. Manet, Ok'Sai (Hokusai), Mind and Ribot," as the poster proclaimed, it marks the beginnings of the modern love of cats and was a great success. It was reprinted twice between October and the end of 1868, and in 1870 there was a second *de luxe* edition enhanced with original prints. For this Manet produced an aquatint of a cat sniffing a jardinière on a balcony.

Manet's unfinished sketch of Mme Manet with a cat on her lap was one of many in a new vogue. Renoir painted a number of such portraits as well as other paintings combining woman and cat (**30**). In the previous century, only children could be portrayed with a cat without a slur on their character: on her virtue if a woman, on his masculinity if a man. Renoir's portrayals may be condescending; they are not intended to be derogatory. Gwen John repeatedly portrayed a young woman with a cat on her lap: it might be called her chosen motif (**31**). And far from being condescending, her paintings have a noble air.

Nonetheless, even these portraits maintain the long established association of cat and woman. And though men had in earlier times kept cats as pets, and scholars and poets, in particular, had not been ashamed to admit the affection they felt for them, until this century men were not portrayed with a favorite cat, in the way that it had long been the convention to be portrayed with a favorite dog. Even when, in the early years of this century, Pierre Bonnard painted two portraits of the dealer

29 Edouard Manet
Reclining woman in Spanish costume, 1862
Oil on canvas, 95 × 114 cm
New Haven, Yale University Art Gallery
Though the cat appears casual enough in this picture, it had a significant role to play both in the poetry of Manet's friend Baudelaire and in Manet's notorious *Olympia*, painted shortly afterwards. So it is likely that even at this date, in the later 19th century, the aura of sin and sensuality still hung like a perfume round the cat.

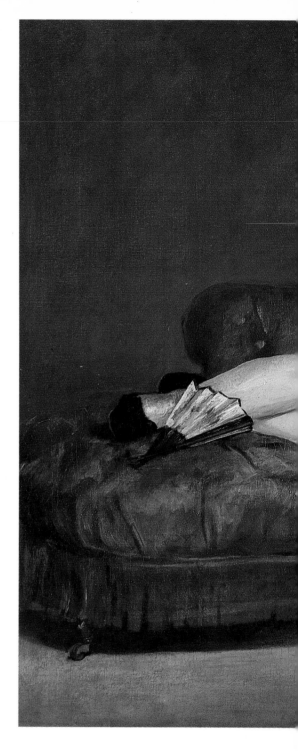

30 Pierre Auguste Renoir
Girl with a cat, c1875
Oil on canvas, 56 × 46.5 cm
Washington, National Gallery of Art

Renoir painted a number of canvases in which a young woman holds a cat on her lap. This is one of the most delightful.

31 Gwen John
Young woman holding a black cat, c1920
Oil on canvas, 47.7 × 29.5 cm
London, Tate Gallery

Gwen John, sister of the flamboyant Augustus, restricted herself to small canvases painted in muted colors. The solemn dignity of this pair of woman and cat examplifies her finest work.

and publisher Ambroise Vollard with a cat on his lap (**32**), the decision must have been made by the artist, for Vollard complained that he had not been able to sleep during the sittings because of the cat. Perhaps the precedent set by Bonnard encouraged his friend Edouard Vuillard to paint the old and eminent writer and publicist of the Impressionists, Théodore Duret, with a cat on his lap (**33**). This was Vuillard's first portrait commission, in 1912, for an agreed fee of 2,000 francs. But Duret was sufficiently pleased with the result to pay 2,500 francs.

32 Pierre Bonnard
Portrait of Ambroise Vollard, 1904–05
Oil on canvas, 74 × 92.5 cm
Zurich, Kunsthaus
Ambroise Vollard, art dealer and publisher of fine art books, sat for a number of artists, most notably for a fine Cubist portrait by Picasso.

33 Edouard Vuillard
Théodore Duret in his study, 1912
Oil on cardboard, 95 × 74.6 cm
Washington, National Gallery of Art, Chester Dale collection
By the time Théodore Duret commissioned this portrait from Vuillard, he was an eminent critic and man of letters.

Cats on their own

Only a little more than a century ago few painters would have thought of painting a cat in isolation. Seventeenth-century Netherlandish kitchen and market pieces were still lifes in which a cat was appropriate. Even painters specializing in animal subjects rarely painted cats. For a painter with larger ambitions, the notion of painting a serious and independent picture of a cat would not have come to mind. Today it is easy to overlook the originality of such paintings as Bonnard's *The white cat* (**34**). Gwen Johns's watercolors, among the finest drawings of a cat, appear to have been done simply to satisfy herself and out of love of the animal (**35**).

In an earlier time, Franz Marc might have been a specialist painter of animals. Shortly before the First World War, in Munich, where he was an associate of Kandinsky in the Blaue Reiter group, he had greater ambitions. "Is there a more mysterious idea for an artist than to imagine how nature is reflected in the eyes of an animal? How does a horse see the world, how does an eagle, a doe, or a dog? It is a poverty-stricken convention to place animals into landscapes as seen by men; instead, we should contemplate the soul of the animal to divine its way of sight." Marc drew and painted animals incessantly in a short career ended by the war, and it is not surprising that he produced two dozen or so drawings, paintings, and prints of cats, of great variety (**36**). Nevertheless, in his theoretical essay already quoted, he does not directly refer to cats. Instead, he asks:"Who is able to paint the existence of a dog as Picasso paints the existence of a cubic shape?"

When Picasso did paint a cat, in 1939, he painted a savage beast (**37**). Like the Roman mosaicist, he shows it with a bird. But where

34   Pierre Bonnard
The white cat, 1894
Oil on cardboard, 51.5 × 33 cm
Paris, Musée d'Orsay

Before the 20th century, paintings of cats by themselves and for themselves, as portraits or studies, are extremely rare. It is perhaps appropriate that this work should come from a leading painter of the movement called "Intimisme", which took as its subject the quiet, intimate moments of bourgeois domestic life, especially as it was lived in the sitting room.

35   Gwen John
The cat, 1905–08
Watercolor on paper, 11.1 × 13.7 cm
London, Tate Gallery

Gwen John, made many watercolors of her
she-cat named Edgar Quinet, after the street in
Paris where she then lived, and was most
distressed when she disappeared. She wrote in
verse: "I never felt your superior, little
mysterious soul in the body of a cat."

36 Franz Marc
Three cats, 1913
Oil on canvas, 72 × 101 cm
Düsseldorf, Kunstsammlung Nordrhein-Westfalen

the Roman cat is a small, pretty creature starting guiltily at being discovered stealing from the kitchen, Picasso's cat is a monster fiercer than a tiger, with extended claws and a quasi-human mask for a face. He then painted a second version, even more horrible, that holds down its prey with claws like boar's teeth and rends the screaming bird with the fanged jaws of a demon or the mouth of Hell itself. The second, more artificial version, he sold: the first, dated 22.4.39, he kept to the end of his life. In their ferocity these two cats recall the brutal bull and the writhing, dying horse Picasso had painted in May 1937 in *Guernica*, his response to the Fascist bombing of the village of Guernica, the worst atrocity of the Spanish Civil War. At that time, for over eighteen months, apart from a few still lifes, Picasso had painted almost nothing but single figures, almost all female and a large majority in the form of a head and shoulders portrait. The two murderous cats follow rapidly on the end of the Spanish Civil War, officially announced on 2 April, and the almost universal international recognition of Franco's Fascist regime by 20 April, which also marked Hitler's fiftieth birthday.

Poor cats! These small, short-lived creatures, content to live in the margins of our lives as once they lived in the margins of psalters, have seldom been granted their own lives. Instead they have been worshipped as gods, feared as infernal, seen as symbols of the dangerously carnal and, today, established in the modern pantheon of idols: pin-ups for those too old for Disney and unsympathetic to the stars of rock and pop. Which painter has been able to paint the existence of a cat?

37   Pablo Picasso
Cat killing a bird, 1939
Oil on canvas, 81 × 100 cm
Antibes, Picasso Museum

Picasso's two paintings of fierce cats may
reflect his reactions to world events, but they
also reflect his obsession, revealed in other
paintings, with his rival mistresses of that
period, Dora Maar and Marie-Thérèse Walter.